Brian Gagg

Robin Hood

Ausmalbuch

Bibliografische Information der Deutschen Nationalbibliothek:
Die Deutsche Nationalbibliothek verzeichnet diese Publikation in der Deutschen
Nationalbibliografie; detaillierte bibliografische
Daten sind im Internet über http://dnb.dnb.de abrufbar.
© 2020 Brian Gagg; 1. Auflage
Covergrafik, Texte & Illustrationen © 2020 Brian Gagg
Herstellung und Verlag: BoD – Books on Demand, Norderstedt
ISBN: 9783751922463

Robin Hood · meeteth · the · tall
Stranger · on · the · Bridge

The.Sheriff.of.Nottingham.cometh.before.the.King.at.London

The·Aged·Palmer·gives·Yovng·David· of·Doncaster·news·of·Will·Stvtely

Little·John·overcomes·Eric·o'·Lincoln

The·Mighty·Fight·betwixt:
Little John· and·the·Cook:

The·stout·bout·between·Little·Iohn·&· Arthvr·a·Bland:·

Merry·Robin·ſtops·a·Stranger·
in·Scarlet :·

The·Four·Yeomen·haue·Merry·
Sport·with·a·Stout·Miller:·

Allan a Dale lieth beside the Fountain

The Merry Friar sings a goodly song

Robin·Hood·Aeps·betwixt·
Sir·Stephen·and·his·Bride:

Merry·Robin·stops·a·Sorrowful·Knight·

Sir·Richard·pleadeth·before·the·Prior·of·Emmet·

ALLAN·A·DALE·SINGETH·BEFORE·OVR·GOOD·QVEEN·ELEANOR·

·MDCCCXXCIII·

Stout·Robin·hath·a·narrow·escape:

RobinHood
slayeth
Guy
of
Gisbourne.

Merry·Robin· hath·the· worst·of· a· Bargain·

AZRAEL

Robin·ſhooteth·his·Laſt·Shaft:

ROBIN·and·LITTLE·JOHN·go·their·ways·in·search·of·Adventure:

Weitere Ausmalbücher von Brian Gagg:

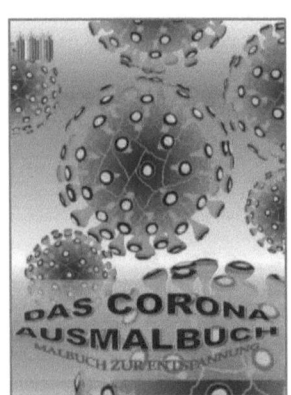

Das Corona
Ausmalbuch

Das Ausmalbuch für
Battle Royale Fans
(Fortnite)

Das Ausmalbuch
für Minecraft Fans